LEGENDS OF WARFARE

AVIATION

P-47 Thunderbolt

Republic's Mighty "Jug" in World War II

DAVID DOYLE

SCHIFFER MILITARY

4880 Lower Valley Road   Atglen, PA 19310

Designed by Justin Watkinson
Type set in Impact/Minion Pro/Univers LT Std
Front cover photo courtesy of Rich Kolasa.

ISBN: 978-0-7643-5673-5
Printed in China

Published by Schiffer Publishing, Ltd.
4880 Lower Valley Road
Atglen, PA 19310
Phone: (610) 593-1777; Fax: (610) 593-2002
E-mail: Info@schifferbooks.com
www.schifferbooks.com

For our complete selection of fine books on this and related subjects, please visit our website at www.schifferbooks.com. You may also write for a free catalog.

Schiffer Publishing's titles are available at special discounts for bulk purchases for sales promotions or premiums. Special editions, including personalized covers, corporate imprints, and excerpts, can be created in large quantities for special needs. For more information, contact the publisher.

We are always looking for people to write books on new and related subjects. If you have an idea for a book, please contact us at proposals@schifferbooks.com.

Acknowledgments

As with all of my projects, this book would not have been possible without the generous help of many friends—some old, some new. Specifically, Tom Kailbourn, Rich Kolasa, Stan Piet, the late Roger Freeman, Dana Bell, and Scott Taylor. Special thanks are owed to Brett Stolle of the National Museum of the United States Air Force. I am especially indebted to my wonderful wife, Denise, for her love as well as her help and support with this project.

Contents

Introduction

Among the iconic aircraft of World War II, the Republic P-47 Thunderbolt not only was physically the biggest single-engine fighter, it also had an enormous impact on history.

P-47s were flown by 132 US Army Air Force squadrons during the Second World War, but they were not flown only by Americans. The aircraft also served with sixteen British Royal Air Force squadrons and four French squadrons, as well as Brazilian, Chinese, and Mexican squadrons attached to US units. The Soviet air force also prominently flew Thunderbolts, though the exact number of squadrons equipped with the massive fighter is uncertain.

In terms of their combat effectiveness, P-47 fliers destroyed 7,067 hostile aircraft, with about half of those "kills" recorded during aerial combat and half destroyed on the ground. Thunderbolt pilots reported destroying 6,000 enemy tanks, 68,000 trucks, 86,000 railway cars, and 9,000 locomotives. For a single-engine fighter, such a tally is definitely one for the history books.

The Thunderbolt grew out of the all-metal, monoplane P-35 design advanced by Alexander Kartveli, chief engineer at Seversky Aircraft Company in the 1930s. Power for the P-35, with its semielliptical wing, came from a Pratt & Whitney R-1830-9 Twin Wasp fourteen-cylinder radial engine.

The Air Corps contracted with Seversky for the P-35 as a new pursuit aircraft, but as it turned out, only seventy-six of the planes were actually produced. Seversky, as it happened, also secretly contracted in 1938 to sell two-seat P-35s to the Japanese navy. Under the designation A8V1, twenty of the planes served Japanese forces in their war in China, a campaign viewed by the American public as a war of naked aggression. Although the United States was still a neutral bystander in the Pacific at that time, the sale aroused ill feeling with respect to the P-35 contract. For their part, the Japanese soon phased out the aircraft too, regarding it as heavy and clumsy.

Although White Russian émigré Alexander de Seversky was an accomplished aviation pioneer who had lost a leg as a combat pilot with the Imperial Russian Navy in World War I, and although he was blessed with effective sales skills, de Seversky's business was foundering in the late 1930s—one of the reasons for the secret Seversky deal with the then-unpopular Japanese military. In 1938, Paul Moore stepped in to rescue the company, but the help came with some tough conditions. Moore required cuts in de Seversky's personal budget. De Seversky's powers were further limited by the board of directors. Then in October 1939, de Seversky was completely ousted from the firm he had founded, and Wallace Kellett took over as president of the company, now renamed Republic Aviation.

Although the restructuring that gave birth to Republic Aviation saw the departure of its Russian émigré founder, his colleague and fellow immigrant from the Russian Empire, chief engineer Alexander Kartveli, remained with Republic. Already in 1939, he came up with the Republic AP-4 model aircraft in answer to an Air Corps request for a new fighter design. Given the experimental designation XP-41, it was bested by the Curtiss P-40, but the Air Corps appreciated Kartveli's design and asked for thirteen improved versions of his aircraft, which was now designated the YP-43.

With its supercharged Pratt & Whitney Twin Wasp engine, the YP-43, now nicknamed the "Lancer," had a phenomenal ceiling of 38,000 feet, prompting an Air Corps order for 272 of the planes. By the fall of 1939, however, all the leading countries of Europe and Asia were at war, and the US Army Air Corps was already looking for an even more powerful airplane, even before the first of Kartveli's aircraft could be delivered. The Air Corps announced a new competition for a pursuit plane in June 1940, and in September—just as Kartveli's first P-43A was being delivered—a conference convened at Wright Field, Ohio, to draft new specifications. The Army's demands were steep: a minimum of 2,000 horsepower, a minimum of six .50-caliber machine guns, a maximum speed of higher than 400 mph, and a ceiling above 40,000 feet. Kartveli went back to work.

The Republic YP-43 was the immediate predecessor of the Republic P-47. Aft of the cockpit was a razorback fairing. This feature would carry over to the early P-47s. Power was provided by a turbosupercharged Pratt & Whitney R-1830-35 engine rated at 1,200 horsepower for takeoff and 1,100 horsepower at 20,000 feet. The first of the thirteen YP-43s was delivered in September 1940. *Stan Piet collection*

Immediately after the Army Air Corps' June 1940 announcement, Republic's Alexander Kartveli began working on a new design. Within Republic his efforts were known as the Advanced Pursuit Design 10, or AP-10. The new aircraft was laid out around the Allison V-1710—a liquid-cooled V-12 engine that was very popular with the Air Corps at the time and was often specified by the service.

After the September Army specifications were announced, Kartveli realized that not only would his initial AP-10, or XP-47, fall short of the new criteria, the same could be said for his second design, the XP-47A, as well.

While the Army had ordered flying prototypes of the XP-47 and XP-47A in November 1939 and January 1940, respectively, Kartveli returned to the drawing board. This time he discarded the V-1710 in favor of the Pratt & Whitney XR-2800 Twin Wasp, then the most powerful engine available. Unlike the sleek, liquid-cooled V-1710, the XR-2800 was a massive, air-cooled twin-row, eighteen-cylinder radial. The engine was rated at over 2,000 horsepower at 28,000 feet, power that Kartveli harnessed with a 12-foot, 2-inch Curtiss Electric C542S four-blade propeller.

In order for the big prop to clear the ground, the aircraft stood 12 feet, 4$^{11}/_{16}$ inches tall. Stretching out behind it was a fuselage that was 35 feet, 4$^3/_{16}$ inches long, to which were attached wings spanning 40 feet, 9$^5/_{16}$ inches. Inside those wings Kartveli planned to enclose eight .50-caliber machine guns, four on each side.

In August 1940, the Army issued a change order, canceling their previously ordered XP-47 and XP-47A prototypes and ordering instead a flying prototype of the R-2800-powered design, which was designated XP-47B.

Less than ten months after that change order was issued, on May 6 1941, the first and only XP-47B lifted off for its first flight. Assigned Army serial number 40-3051, the aircraft soon proved itself, meeting or exceeding all the September 1940 design requirements. C. Hart Miller of Republic Aviation dubbed the new aircraft "Thunderbolt."

Pleased with the initial flight test results, the Army Air Corps soon ordered five YP-47B service test aircraft, to be followed by 165 production examples.

The first Thunderbolt, the XP-47B, was lost on August 8, 1942, when the supercharger exhaust ignited the partially retracted tailwheel. The fire spread, leading pilot Fillmore "Fil" Gilmer to bail out. Gilmore parachuted to safety, landing in Long Island Sound. The XP-47B also landed in the sound and was destroyed.

While XP-47 and XP-47A aircraft were designed, it was the XP-47B design that formed the basis for the famed fighter. Designer Alexander Kartveli, drawing on lessons learned from the recent Battle of Britain, laid out an aircraft incorporating more horsepower, weapons, and armor than found in previous US fighters. Assembly of a prototype XP-47B was contracted for by the US Army Air Corps on September 6, 1940. The aircraft was assigned serial number 40-3051. *Stan Piet collection*

Lowry Brabham, chief test pilot of Republic Aviation, opens the hinged cockpit door of the XP-47B before its first flight on May 6, 1941. That flight was brief, since smoke caused by an oil leak entered the cockpit. The cockpit door was found only on the left side of the prototype. *Stan Piet collection*

The oil leak was repaired, and flight testing of the XP-47B resumed. Performance of the massive new fighter impressed the Army Air Corps. Here the aircraft soars over Long Island. *Stan Piet collection*

CHAPTER 2
P-47B

On Thursday, November 27, 1941, Republic's facility in Farmingdale, New York, turned out the first preproduction Thunderbolt, YP-47B, with serial number 41-5895. Ten days later came the Japanese attack on Pearl Harbor, and two weeks after that, on Sunday, December 21, the government accepted the aircraft. Republic put together four more of the preproduction YP-47B before finishing, on April 3, 1942, the first production version of the P-47B, serial number 41-5900.

Some two months later, in June 1942, Thunderbolts were arriving at the Bridgeport, Connecticut, base of the 56th Fighter Group, and it was not long before serious problems arose. In only two weeks, about half the planes had crashed. In high-speed, high-altitude dive tests, pilots found the aircraft's control surfaces to be unresponsive. Eighteen Thunderbolt pilots were lost before the cause of the phenomenon—known as compressibility—was found and a solution was devised. At low speeds, air compressibility

in the flow over the wing is not significant, but as aircraft near the speed of sound, compressibility increases, potentially with devastating results. The phenomenon was only beginning to be understood in the early 1940s, as aircraft speeds rose higher and higher. Thunderbolt pilots learned to reduce throttle and ride their dives until reaching lower altitudes, where the air was denser and control surfaces would again respond. Pilots had to learn to avoid putting excessive stress on their aircraft by only gently applying pressure to their controls.

As the lessons of coping with compressibility were being absorbed, the 56th Fighter Group (FG) was deployed to Britain in December 1942. The 56th would go on to become one of the most famous and effective P-47 groups, scoring 674.5 aerial victories according to the US Air Force Historical Study No. 84, which also indicates that thirty-nine of the group's pilots became aces while serving with the 56th.

War Department Contract #15850, dated September 13, 1940, had called for the production of 225 P-47 aircraft. Among these were five YP-47B aircraft and 165 full-production versions. The P-47B aircraft were assigned serial numbers 41-5895 to 41-6065. The first of these was delivered to the US Army Air Force (as the US Army Air Corps had been renamed on June 20, 1941) on December 21, 1941.
National Museum of the United States Air Force

Here, P-47B, serial number 41-5931, is shown from above. Painted borders surround the access doors for the main fuel filler (at the lower front of the windscreen) as well as the auxiliary fuel tank filler cap (above the wing root). *National Archives*

At the center of the P-47B cockpit was the control stick, with rudder pedals on either side and ahead. To the left of the pilot was the main electrical panel. The cutout at the top of the instrument panel was typical of several P-47 models. Various gauges provide information about the aircraft's attitude and the performance of the Pratt & Whitney R-2800-21 engine. *American Aviation Historical Society*

In the foreground of this group of Thunderbolts is P-47B, serial number 41-5963. Visible is the heavily scalloped, well-defined demarcation between the upper camouflage color, Olive Drab, and the lower color, Neutral Gray. The forward rake of the radio mast, characteristic of the P-47B, is apparent on all the aircraft in this 1942 photograph. *National Museum of the United States Air Force*

CHAPTER 3
P-47C

With testing and then actual combat underway, development of the Thunderbolt did not stop with the introduction of the P-47B. When the P-47C made its debut in mid-1942, it already incorporated new radio equipment that included the first use of a vertical antenna mast on a Thunderbolt. The aircraft's turbosupercharger was refined and the elevators now had added internal counterweights that helped pilots cope with the compressibility issue in recovering from high-speed dives.

Four production blocks of the P-47C were built: the P-47C-RE, P-47C-1-RE, P-47C-2-RE, and P-47C-5-RE, the suffix RE standing for Republic's facility in Farmingdale, Long Island.

Externally, the fifty-seven P-47C-RE aircraft appeared almost identical to the earlier P-47B; only the antenna looked different. On September 14, 1942, however, the first of 112 P-47C-1RE aircraft began rolling off the assembly line, and these planes looked distinctly different. C-1 Thunderbolts featured the Quick Engine Change or QEC package. To fit the new engine mounting, 8 inches were added in front of the aircraft's firewall, and thus the total length of the plane grew to 36 feet, 1 inch.

Ironically, despite all the impressive improvements, none of the C-1 Thunderbolts (which started with serial number 41-6066)

nor any of the P-47C-RE aircraft would serve in combat. The first "C" to engage the enemy was P-47C-2-RE, an aircraft that also featured a four-point suspension system and a reinforced fuselage keel that allowed it to carry added ordnance or external fuel tanks—both of which would be of tremendous importance.

A total of 300 P-47C-5-RE Thunderbolts followed the 128 P-47C-2-RE planes, beginning with serial number 41-6178. It was with the P-47C that the Thunderbolt acquired its famous nickname—the "Jug." According to legend, upon receiving orders to switch from the Supermarine Spitfire to the bulbous Republic aircraft, incredulous 4th FG pilots exclaimed, "Why, it looks like a milk jug!"

The sleek, maneuverable Spitfire looked every bit a cutting-edge fighter aircraft, and it performed like one too—with its liquid-cooled Rolls-Royce Merlin engine and its light weight: 2.3 tons.

Looks aren't everything, however, and despite weighing nearly twice as much as the iconic British fighter, the P-47C was powered by a sturdy R-2800 radial engine that could take a beating, and it was armed with eight Browning .50-caliber machine guns, as compared with the Spitfire's eight .303 Brownings or four .303 Brownings and two 20 mm cannon.

The P-47C superseded the P-47B and featured an improved GE turbosupercharger, all-metal control surfaces, and a redesigned oxygen system. The radio equipment was revised as well and now had a vertically mounted antenna, rather than the raked antenna of the P-47B. This P-47C, serial number 41-6530, VM-A, was assigned to the 551st Fighter Training Squadron, Atcham, United Kingdom, in 1944. *Stan Piet collection*

"Betty" has been painted just beneath "51" on the cowling of P-47C-RE, serial number 41-6086. This aircraft was the subject of an October 24, 1942, photo study that illustrates the characteristics of this production block. The initial P-47C production, P-47C-REs, can be distinguished from later P-47C models by the lack of the 8-inch-wide extension in the fuselage to the front of the cockpit, aft of the louvers, which were characteristic of the later models. *National Archives*

On the side of the fuselage of "Betty," to the front of the national insignia, is visible the left intercooler door. The forward-slanting stripe painted to the rear of the national insignia indicates that this aircraft is the "B" flight leader. *National Museum of the United States Air Force*

Viewed from the front, the ovoid shape of the cowling of P-47C-RE, serial number 41-6086, is apparent. Barrels of six of the eight .50-caliber machine guns are visible protruding from the wings. *National Archives*

The second group of the P-47C aircraft was the P-47C-2-RE production block. Thunderbolt 41-6182, photographed at Bovingdon in January 1943, was part of that block. The national insignia on this aircraft, the fourth P-47 to arrive in the United Kingdom, has a yellow surround. *National Museum of the United States Air Force*

The P-47C was used in combat, as is evident with P-47C-2-RE, serial number 41-6235. The aircraft, which was assigned to Lt. Robert S. Johnson of the 61st Fighter Squadron, 56th Fighter Group, was attacked by a Focke-Wulf Fw 190 in June 1943. The Focke-Wulf scored a hit behind the canopy with its 20 mm cannon. Fortunately, despite the proximity to the cockpit, the pilot as well as the Thunderbolt survived. *National Museum of the United States Air Force*

CHAPTER 4

P-47D and G Razorback

Not surprisingly, demand for combat aircraft went through the roof once the United States was fully involved in a world war on three separate continents at once.

Demand for the P-47 far exceeded the capacity of Republic's factory in Farmingdale, New York. Accordingly, work on a new assembly plant in Evansville, Indiana, was begun on April 7, 1942, and the first Indiana Thunderbolt rolled off that assembly line less than six months later on September 20, in a vivid example of the World War II spirit of "We can do it!"

Another way in which the exploding demand for "Jugs" was dealt with was through licensing production of the P-47 to Curtiss. This not only served to increase deliveries of the needed P-47s but also was something of a consolation prize for Curtiss, whose contract for a radial-powered fighter of their own design, the P-60A, had been canceled.

The 334 Curtiss-built P-47Ds—as well as twenty clones of P-47Cs—were designated P-47G. Thus, only a unique model number would distinguish the Curtiss-built "Jugs" from their Republic-built siblings.

The Thunderbolts built in Indiana by Republic shared model numbers with their Farmingdale-produced sisters, being distinguished only by their block number suffixes: while RE designated P-47s built in Farmingdale, New York, RA indicated a plane constructed in Evansville, Indiana.

Externally, the P-47D closely resembled the P-47C, since most of the changes were on the inside of the aircraft. Improvement was a constant throughout the years the P-47 was produced, and new production blocks signified the introduction of major innovations.

The B-7 shackle was introduced on the P-47D-6-RE. The shackle, fitted under the fuselage, allowed the aircraft to carry either a 500-pound bomb or a 200-gallon ferry tank.

A new, more powerful engine, the R-2800-63, made its debut in the P-47D-10-RE and P-47D-11-RA. This power plant featured water injection and a new turbosupercharger that increased horsepower to 2,300 when put at the war emergency setting. Internal fuel capacity was raised on the P-47D-15 block, which also incorporated more B-7 shackles—one under each wing, enabling the aircraft to carry even more bombs or drop tanks.

A new propeller, the Hamilton Standard 24E50-65 13-foot, 1⅞-inch four-bladed prop, replaced the earlier Curtiss Electric C542S propeller on the P-47D-22-RE built in Farmingdale. Meanwhile the plant in Evansville was switching to the Curtiss Electric C542S-A114 prop, also with a 13-foot diameter, on the P-47D-23-RA aircraft.

The P-47D was truly a mass-produced aircraft, with 12,602 examples being built. However, not all P-47Ds were alike. In fact, many changes were to be made during the production run. Just a few of those changes include bubble canopies and lowered rear decks, a bulged fuselage keel with equipment for mounting a fuel tank or bomb, various propellers, water injection, extra cowl flaps, wing pylons, rocket-launching stubs, and different types of propellers. This aircraft, P-47D-22-RE, serial number 42-26293, piloted by Lt. Arnold A. Laflam of the 63rd Fighter Squadron, 56th Fighter Group, was named "Belle of Belmont." Beneath Belle of Belmont's wings are two different styles of 150-gallon drop tank. *US Air Force Academy*

This aircraft is said to be one of four preproduction P-47Ds produced by Republic's Evansville, Indiana, plant. That plant delivered its first Thunderbolt, serial number 42-22250, on October 23, 1942. *National Archives*

In 1940–41, Curtiss-Wright had hoped to update their P-40 design into something that would remain relevant at the time. The project became the XP-60, which went through multiple iterations before being canceled. In order to continue utilizing the Curtiss-Wright plant space in Buffalo, New York, for war production, the company was awarded a contract to license production of the Thunderbolt, using the designation P-47G. The first twenty aircraft were similar to the Republic P-47C, but the remainder of the 354 P-47Gs were equivalent to P-47Ds. *National Museum of the United States Air Force*

This P-47G is photographed in June 1943, six months into Curtiss's production of the type. The final P-47G rolled off the Curtiss assembly line in March 1944. *National Museum of the United States Air Force*

Serial number 42-24958 was a Curtiss P-47G-1-CU Thunderbolt. This aircraft was damaged in a landing accident on January 21, 1944, at Page Field, Fort Myers, Florida. Most of the P-47G aircraft were used in stateside training roles. *National Museum of the United States Air Force*

This war-weary (as denoted by the "WW" stenciled on the tail) P-47D-1-RE, serial number 42-7922, was assigned to Detachment B, which was later renamed the 5th Emergency Rescue Squadron. The D-1-RE production block featured two additional cowl flaps on each side, below what previously had been the bottom flap. *Stan Piet collection*

A fairing for mounting an RDF loop antenna is visible aft of the cockpit canopy of P-47D-2-RE, serial number 42-8009. The aircraft, which was damaged beyond repair in a crash at Wright Field, Ohio, on March 5, 1945, wears pre–June 1943 national insignia in this photo. *National Museum of the United States Air Force*

The first production block of Thunderbolts built at Republic's plant in Evansville, Indiana, P-47D-1-RA, consisted of 110 aircraft, including this one, serial number 42-22286. While the suffix RE was for aircraft manufactured at Farmingdale, the suffix RA denoted Evansville-built aircraft. *Stan Piet collection*

A steam cleaner is being used to remove preservatives from this P-47D, freshly arrived via ship, in Townsville, Australia. The propeller and guns will be installed in due course. This P-47D has the early-type additional cowl flaps, with the trailing edges even with those of the cowl flaps above them. *National Archives*

Two P-47Ds of the 5th Emergency Rescue Squadron at Boxted, England, are shown in this 1944 view. In the foreground is P-47D-5-RE, serial number 42-8586, with inflatable dinghies to be dropped to downed airmen on the wing pylons, and in the background is "Primrose Peggy," P-47D-5-RE 42-8646. *Stan Piet collection*

The cowling has been removed from this 5th Emergency Rescue Squadron Thunderbolt, P-47D-5-RE, serial number 44-8554. The aircraft is marked with black and white invasion stripes on the fuselage as well as the tops and bottoms of the wings. At left is an M2 Cletrac, and just visible in the hangar is a second P-47. *US Air Force Academy*

Visible on this Thunderbolt is the bulged keel along with mountings for a bomb or drop tank, features that became standard with the P-47D-5-RE. *Stan Piet collection*

Lt. Warren F. Penny flew this P-47D-10-RE, serial number 42-75007. Nicknamed "Topper," the Thunderbolt and Penny were assigned to the 317th Fighter Squadron, 325th Fighter Group, 15th Air Force, in San Pancrazio, Italy. This aircraft was reportedly the only natural-metal-finished P-47D in the 325th Fighter Group—the "Checkertail Clan." *US Air Force Academy*

The Pratt & Whitney R-2800 Twin Wasp radial engine powered all production models of the Thunderbolt. The eighteen-cylinder engine had two rows of nine cylinders, each cylinder with a bore of 5.75 inches and a stroke of 6 inches, giving each cylinder a displacement of 155.8 cubic inches and the engine a total displacement of 2,804.5 cubic inches. The displacement and radial configuration resulted in the model designation R-2800. The engine was designed to run on 100/130 octane gasoline. The extensive use of aluminum and other lightweight metals held the weight of the 53-inch-diameter engine to 2,360 pounds. *National Museum of the United States Air Force*

The black object atop the rear of the R-2800 is the carburetor. While Pratt & Whitney designed the R-2800 and was the first to place it in production, at their plant in East Hartford, Connecticut, wartime demand for the engine was so great that not only was this augmented by a new Pratt & Whitney plant, located in Kansas City, Missouri, but also production was licensed to Chevrolet in Tonawanda, New York; Ford Motor Company in Dearborn, Michigan; and Nash-Kelvinator, who first built the engines in Lansing, Michigan, and later in Kenosha, Wisconsin. *National Museum of the United States Air Force*

In the Pacific, P-47D-15-RE, serial number 42-75786, "Noble Norma," flew with the 19th Fighter Squadron, 318th Fighter Group. This group made considerable use of the P-47D type in ground attack missions before converting to P-47Ns in early 1945. *Stan Piet collection*

This P-47D-16-RE, serial number 42-76049, has just jettisoned a Lockheed 165-gallon external fuel tank of the type designed for use on P-38s. The use of drop tanks allowed fighters, including the P-47, to greatly extend their range. Several types of drop tanks were used on Thunderbolts, including a "flat" 150-gallon type and 108-gallon steel or paper types. *National Museum of the United States Air Force*

Ground crewmen from the 61st Fighter Squadron, 56th Fighter Group, are making adjustments to "In the Mood," P-47D-1-RE, serial number 42-7877 (fuselage code HV-D), assigned to Capt. Gerald Johnson. The national insignia used briefly in the summer of 1943 is present. The propeller is the Curtiss Electric, with a diameter of 12 feet, 2 inches. *Imperial War Museum*

The pilot of a Republic P-47 Thunderbolt Mk. II of No. 30 Squadron, Royal Air Force, is entering the cockpit while the engine warms up, prior to a mission out of Jumchar, Burma. The white band on the nose and the white stripes on the wings and the horizontal stabilizers were special friendly-identification markings used by the Southeast Asia Command. The RAF designated its razorback P-47s the Thunderbolt Mk. I, and its bubble-canopy P-47s the Thunderbolt Mk. II. *Imperial War Museum*

Razorback P-47 Thunderbolts from the 83rd Fighter Squadron, 78th Fighter Group, are being prepared for their next mission at RAF Duxford. The cowlings are decorated with the 78th's distinctive black-and-white checkerboard pattern. At the center is "Noamie Vee," P-47D-21-RA serial number 43-25528, code HL-H. The photo predates September 5, 1944, as "Noamie Vee" was damaged in a belly landing at Duxford on that date and, after being patched back together, was transferred to the 36th Fighter Group. Some sources claim that the plane to the right probably was "Green Hornet," P-47D-28-RA, 42-28518, fuselage code HL-C, flown by Capt. Robert T. Green, but this information must be incorrect because the last production block of Republic-Evansville Thunderbolts with the razorback canopy was the P-47D-23-RA. *Roger Freeman collection*

"Blondie II" was P-47D-6-RE, serial number 42-74676, fuselage code CS-X, assigned to the 359th Fighter Group. *Roger Freeman collection*

"Princess Pat," P-47D-10-RE, serial number 42-75185, was flown by 1st Lt. Charles Reed of the 63rd Fighter Squadron, 56th Fighter Group. The photo was taken at RAF Steeple Morden, and the date would have been in or after August 1943, when Reed was assigned to that squadron. This Thunderbolt carried the fuselage code UN-X.

In another view, "Belle of Belmont," previously seen on page 21, shows off the 150-gallon drop tank shackled to the left wing pylon. *US Air Force Academy*

This P-47D-22-RE, serial number 42-26298, fuselage code LM-A, flown by Lt. Albert A. Knafelz of the 62nd Fighter Squadron, 56th Fighter Group, operated under various names, including "Button Nose" and "Stalag Luft III/I Wanted Wings." The artwork on the nose shows Donald Duck behind bars. *US Air Force Academy*

War-weary P-47D-23 RA, serial number 42-27606, was modified into two-seat configuration, featuring a shortened front canopy and a bubble canopy for the rear seat. Dubbed "Lady Helen," the Thunderbolt was used as a VIP transport by the 78th Fighter Group, known as the "Duxford Eagles," during late World War II. *Stan Piet collection*

A column of razorback Republic Thunderbolts of No. 30 Squadron are taxiing past rows of British Hawker Hurricane Mk. IICs at Cox's Bazaar, India, during World War II. Each Thunderbolt is carrying two 165-gallon drop tanks on the wing pylons. The Thunderbolts and the Hurricanes had small roundels under the wings, and the Thunderbolts had white bands on the cowlings. *Imperial War Museum*

Two P-47s from the 63rd Fighter Squadron, 56th Fighter Group, are parked near a stockpile of drop tanks. The ones painted gray in the foreground were fabricated from sheet metal, while the silver-colored ones in the right background were a type invented by the British, made of compressed kraft paper impregnated with resorcinol glue. *Roger Freeman collection*

This P-47D, wearing *Luftwaffe* markings, was recaptured by Allied forces at a German base in Göttingen, Germany. The bottom and tail of the Thunderbolt had been painted yellow, and German crosses had been applied. *National Archives*

A second canopy, seat, and pilot controls were added forward of the normal pilot's position of P-47G-15-CU 42-25266, creating the two place TP-47G. Dubbed the "Doublebolt," 42-25266, and similarly modified 42-25267, were the only two aircraft converted in this manner at the factory, although a handful of aircraft were modified in a similar fashion in the field. *Republic archives via LIRAHS*

Above the right rudder pedal of the P-47D is a panel with the blinker oxygen-flow indicator, supply warning light, and oxygen-cylinder gauge. At lower left in this photo can be seen the throttle quadrant. *National Museum of the United States Air Force*

In another view of a P-47D cockpit, various instruments and controls can be clearly seen, including the parking-brake control directly ahead of the stick. Above the stick, in the cutout at the top of the panel, is a placard indicating safe diving speeds. *National Archives*

On the left side of the cockpit of this P-47D, the box-shaped grip used on the P-47D-5-RE and P-47D-10-RE throttle handle can be seen. Aft of the throttle quadrant are the landing-gear control and trim-tab controls, while in the foreground is the pilot's seat and the control stick. *National Museum of the United States Air Force*

In later-production P-47Ds, the elevator trim-tab control wheel as seen in the previous photo was replaced by an elevator trim-tab hand crank, partially hidden by the side of the seat at the lower center of this photo. The fuel selector valve is visible at lower right. *National Archives*

This P-47 seems to be undergoing maintenance for a number of issues. The sliding canopy has been removed, a mechanic (seen in the shade of the wing) is working on the right main landing gear, and the cowling has been removed, revealing the R-2800 engine. *US Air Force Academy*

Maintenance and operating procedures for the R-2800 call for the engine to be overhauled after 2,000–3,000 hours of operation. Here, mechanics of the 386th Air Service Squadron on the Lingayen Airstrip, Luzon, Philippines, are removing the engine from a P-47D on April 27, 1945. *National Archives*

Because of the huge amount of dust at the Lingayen Airstrip, mechanics of the 386th Air Service Squadron, which was based there, had to pull the cowlings and clean the engines of the squadron's P-47s daily, rather than at the prescribed twenty-five-flying-hour intervals. Here, dust is being removed from the engine and its accessories. *National Archives*

Two armorers load .50-caliber ammunition into the four ammo bays inside each wing of the P-47, while a third armorer cleans one of the gun barrels. The maximum load of ammunition was 425 rounds per gun, but if all eight machine guns were to be loaded for a mission, this was reduced to 200 rounds per gun, equivalent to about thirteen seconds of fire. Thus, pilots typically fired only short bursts. *National Museum of the United States Air Force*

Armorers reload a P-47 at a captured airfield in Normandy on June 15, 1944, only nine days after the invasion. In the background, a GI rests on one of scores of captured Jerry cans.
National Archives

This 353rd Fighter Group P-47 in England is loaded with an array of bombs, including a general-purpose bomb in the center and inverted-V-shaped racks holding twenty-four small fragmentation bombs, arranged in two rows of twelve bombs each.
National Archives

In preparation of test firing, an M2 tractor supports the tail of this 12th Air Force P-47D in Italy, positioning the airplane in flight attitude. Armors attend to the triple-tube 4.5-inch rocket launchers. *National Archives*

One armorer slides a 4.5-inch rocket into a launcher while another holds the next rocket. After removing the rockets from their packing tubes, they were inspected for damage prior to having fuses installed. Once in the launcher, the contact arms were engaged, allowing the firing circuit to be completed by the pilot. *National Archives*

The triple-tube 4.5-inch rocket launchers under each wing allowed a P-47 to fire a volley comparable to six 105 mm high-explosive shells, which had a maximum range of approximately 4,600 yards. *National Archives*

Two basic types of fin-stabilized 4.5-inch rockets were used: the M9 practice round and the M8 high-explosive rocket. Here, an armorer performs a final check of connections to the rockets. *National Archives*

The Chinese Nationalist air force was furnished a number of P-47s during the post–World War II Chinese Civil War, including this one, P-47D-23-RA, serial number 42-27730. *Stan Piet collection*

A razorback P-47D bearing the nickname "Snafu" (*left*) and fuselage code WZ-D, to replicate a plane in the 84th Fighter Squadron, 78th Fighter Group, 8th Air Force, and another P-47D (*right*) with fuselage code UN-I, to replicate a plane in the 63rd Fighter Squadron, 56th Fighter Group, are parked together at an airshow. *Rich Kolasa*

"Snafu" is also marked with another nickname, "War Eagle," with an emblem of a diving eagle wearing a red, white, and blue top hat and clutching a swastika in its claws. This restored Thunderbolt is marked to replicate the original "Snafu / War Eagle," P-47D-6-RE, serial number 42-74742, from the 84th Fighter Squadron, which was written off after a crash landing at RAF Duxford on December 15, 1944. This plane now flies under civil registration number NX47FG. *Rich Kolasa*

In a left-rear view of "Snafu" with its engine warming up, a round rear-view mirror is visible above the windscreen. The frame of the sliding canopy is silver colored. Black and white invasion stripes are painted on the fuselage and the wings. These stripes were an identification aid on Allied aircraft starting at the time of the June 6, 1944, invasion of Normandy. *Rich Kolasa*

A rear view of "Snafu" demonstrates the rear-visibility issues that pilots experienced with the turtleback P-47s. The bubbletop canopy introduced during P-47D production gave pilots much better visibility in all directions. *Rich Kolasa*

The UHF mast antenna on the turtleback was mounted slightly to the left of the ridge at the top of the turtleback aft of the cockpit. The angle at which the tail-gear doors rested when in the open position is apparent. *Rich Kolasa*

CHAPTER 5
P-47D Bubbletop

The ability to draw a bead on the enemy before he is able to see you has been a key tactical advantage since the beginning of warfare. If anything, this goes double for aerial combat. Pursuit pilots—as fighter pilots were then known—often complained about aircraft features that obstructed their line of sight, and in regard to American pilots in the early days of World War II, their objections tended to focus on two aircraft features. First there was the metal frame that made up aircraft canopies. Second, and specifically on the Thunderbolt, pilots objected to the thick "razorback" that faired the canopy's rear into the fuselage.

In an effort to eliminate the first of these objections on the P-47, the British "Malcolm Hood" began to be installed on Thunderbolts in the field. The Malcolm Hood was a protruding Perspex (Plexiglas) aircraft canopy originally created for the Spitfire by the British R. Malcolm Company, an engineering and production firm producing aircraft components that was based in Berkshire, England. The Malcolm Hood was later adapted to the P-51, and although the wider girth of the P-47 caused some initial difficulties, eventually the hood was adapted for the P-47C and D, giving their pilots an unobstructed field of vision.

Unobstructed, that is, as far as the canopy itself was concerned. The Malcolm Hood failed to deal with the other visibility problem in the P-47; namely, the "razorback" that faired the rear of the cockpit to the rear fuselage. Once more, British technology came to the rescue. As an experiment, a Hawker Typhoon full-bubble canopy was fitted to a P-47, producing an XP-47K (which is addressed later in this book). Tests of the XP-47K produced positive results, and Republic resolved to introduce the bubble canopy on the P-47D, starting with block P-47D-25-RE in Farmingdale and P-47D-26-RA in Evansville.

For a fighter pilot, much of the battle is visibility. Toward that end, Republic experimented with a bubble-type canopy on the XP-47K. Tests were favorable, and beginning with the P-47D-25-RE production block at Farmingdale and the P-47D-26-RA at Evansville, subsequent P-47Ds featured cut-down rear decks and bubble canopies. This P-47D-25-RE, serial number 42-26641, nicknamed "Hairless Joe," was flown by Col. David Schilling, who commanded the 56th Fighter Group from August 1944 to January 1945. "Hairless Joe" is shown here at RAF Boxted / USAAF Station 150, England, in the summer of 1945.
Stan Piet collection

Contrasting the two styles of P-47D, bubbletop "Hairless Joe" warms up next to razorback P-47D-22-RE, serial number 42-26280, "Ugly Duckling" (fuselage code LM-Z), prior to taking off on a mission from Boxted in 1944. *US Air Force Academy*

In another view, eighteen kill marks are visible on the left side of Schilling's "Hairless Joe" at Boxted in the summer of 1945. The bubble canopy could be opened either electrically or manually and was jettisonable in an emergency. *Stan Piet collection*

Two 56th Fighter Group armorers place .50-caliber ammunition in the left-wing ammunition bays of Francis S. "Gabby" Gabreski's P-47D in 1944. Rollers and feed chutes were designed to guide the ammunition to the guns' receivers, which are open here.
National Archives

With sun glistening off their natural-metal finishes, three P-47D-25-REs, including serial number 42-26429, *foreground*, and serial number 42-26428, *center*, fly over water. The internal fuel capacity of the P-47D-25-RE and P-47D-26-RA was increased 65 gallons over that of preceding models, now totaling 370 gallons, with a corresponding increase in range, very important especially in the Pacific. *Stan Piet collection*

The blue cowl ring of this 514th Fighter Squadron, 406th Fighter Group, Ninth Air Force P-47D-26-RA, serial number 42-28401, transitions into a tapering blue marking on the upper fuselage. Blue also adorns the rudder trim tab, and there are red, blue, and yellow stripes on the vertical tail. *Stan Piet collection*

Two P-47D-27-REs with diverse markings form up for a publicity shot. In the foreground, wearing Brazilian markings, is serial number 42-26777, and in the background is a bubbletop P-47 in British markings. *National Museum of the United States Air Force*

Assigned to the 63rd Fighter Squadron, 56th Fighter Group, "Pat," P-47D-28-RA, serial number 42-28543, was shot down near Etten, Holland, on September 9, 1944. The plane, which wore the fuselage code UN-V, was lost, along with the pilot, Capt. Roy T. Fling. *US Air Force Academy*

While the active postwar Air Force did not use the Thunderbolt—a situation many lamented in Korea—the aircraft was a staple of post–World War II Air National Guard units. Here, F-47s and F-82s fill the ramp of a desert air base. In the foreground is F-47D-40-RA, serial number 45-49151, of the 149th Fighter Squadron, far away from its home with the Virginia Air National Guard. The dorsal fins, characteristic of that production block, are painted orange on these Thunderbolts. *Stan Piet collection*

The United States exported large numbers of P-47s to over twenty Allied nations during and after World War II. In this photograph, taken in Peru, a pilot is warming the engine of a bubbletop P-47D Thunderbolt, while a ground crewman stands by with a fire extinguisher in the event of an engine fire. The fuselage bears a partially visible roundel-type national insignia. *American Aviation Historical Society*

In a view of two bubbletop P-47Ds, likely taken at the El Pato Base in Talara-Piura airfield in the 1960s, the nearer plane, numbered 116 on the fuselage, has a roundel national insignia and stripes on the rudder. The Peruvian government received fifty-six P-47Ds, and in the 1960s, enthusiast Ed Jurist purchased six of these and forty tons of spares. This purchase would form the core of the Thunderbolts flying today. *American Aviation Historical Society*

Specifications

	P-47B	P-47C	P-47D	P-47M	P-47N
Dimensions					
Wing span:	40 ft. 9.31 in.	40 ft. 9.31 in.	40 ft. 9.31 in.	40 ft. 9.31 in.	42 ft. 7 in.
Length:	35 ft. 3.25 in.	36 ft. 1.75 in.	36 ft. 1.75 in.	36 ft. 1.75 in.	36 ft. 1. in.
Height:	12 ft. 8 in.	14 ft. 1.75 in.	14 ft. 7 in.	14 ft. 8 in.	14 ft. 8 in.
Wing area:	300 sq. ft.	300 sq. ft.	300 sq. ft.	300 sq. ft.	322 sq. ft.
Weights					
Empty:	9,346 lbs.	9,900 lbs.	10,000 lbs.	10,000 lbs.	11,000 lbs.
Gross:	12,245 lbs.	12,500 lbs.	14,500 lbs.	14,500 lbs.	16,300 lbs.
Max. T/O:	13,360 lbs.	14,925 lbs.	19,400 lbs.	19,400 lbs.	20,700 lbs.
Performance and Equipment					
Max. speed:	429 mph @27,800 ft.	433 mph @ 30,000 ft.	428 mph @ 30,000 ft.	475 mph @ 32,000 ft.	467 mph @ 32,500 ft.
Service ceiling:	42,000 ft.	42,000 ft.	42,000 ft.	41,000 ft.	43,000 ft.
Range:	550 miles	640 miles	475 miles	530 miles	800 miles
Max. range:	1,100 miles	1,250 miles	1,700 miles		2,200 miles
Power plant:	Pratt & Whitney R-2800-21 2,000 hp, turbosupercharged	Pratt & Whitney R-2800-21 2,000 hp, turbosupercharged	Pratt & Whitney R-2800-63 2,000 hp, turbosupercharged	Pratt & Whitney R-2800-57 2,800 hp, turbosupercharged	Pratt & Whitney R-2800-57/-73/-77 2,800 hp, water injected, turbosupercharged
Armament:	8 x .50-cal. machine guns	8 x .50-cal. machine guns One 500 lb. bomb.	8 x .50-cal. machine guns 2,500 lb. bombs or ten 5-in. rockets.	8 x .50-cal. machine guns	8 x .50-cal. machine guns 3,000 lb. bombs or ten 5-in. rockets.
Number built:	170	602 + 20 built as P-47G	12,602 + 334 P-47G	130	1,816

The Lone Star Flight Museum, in Houston, Texas, owns and operates a P-47D painted to replicate "Tarheel Hal," a P-47D-40-RA with the 366th Fighter Squadron, 358th Fighter Group, Ninth Air Force, based at Toul, France, in 1944. This actual plane was a P-47D-40-RA accepted by the Army on May 7, 1945. After World War II, the Venezuelan air force purchased the plane, and it was repatriated to the United States in the early 1990s. The US Air Force assisted with its restoration. The Lone Star Flight Museum acquired the plane in June 1998. *Rich Kolasa*

The "Tarheel Hal" restoration's underside is viewed in flight as it rolls, depicting details of the elliptical wings and the belly of the fuselage. The three teardrop-shaped objects on each of the Frise-type ailerons served as counterweights. *Rich Kolasa*

In a left-rear view of "Tarheel Hal," the bulge on the bottom of the fuselage, below the national insignia, is the supercharger exhaust hood. On the lower part of the trailing edge of the rudder is the tail navigation light. *Rich Kolasa*

Republic P-47D-40-RA, serial number 44-90471, has been restored to flying condition and is painted to replicate Lt. Col. David C. Schilling's aircraft, "Hairless Joe," fuselage code LM-S and serial number 42-26641, from the 62nd Fighter Squadron, 56th Fighter Group, 8th Air Force. After World War II, this Thunderbolt served with the Peruvian air force. It was returned to the United States in 1969 and has had a succession of owners. *Rich Kolasa*

"Hairless Joe" is painted in a dark-gray and olive-green over neutral-gray camouflage scheme. The tail number, 226641, amounted to the serial number, with the first digit, 4, omitted. Under the wings are zero-length launch mounts for 5-inch high-velocity aircraft rockets (HVARs). *Rich Kolasa*

The "Hairless Joe" nose art on the cowling features a white disc, with the cartoon character superimposed: he is carrying a large club and a rock, has a blonde beard and long hair, is wearing a yellow vest with polka dots as well as dark-colored pants with patches on the knees, and is barefooted. *Rich Kolasa*

To the front of the dorsal fin of "Hairless Joe" is a dorsal fin extending forward to the UHF mast antenna. This dorsal fin was introduced beginning with the P-47D-40-RA. The small antennas on the side of the vertical fin are for the AN/APS-13 tail-warning radar, introduced with the P-47D-40-RA. The rudder was sheathed with Alclad aluminum alloy, as were the elevators and the ailerons; fabric cladding was not strong enough to withstand the stresses on the control surfaces during flight. *Rich Kolasa*

In a view of the underside of the right wing of "Hairless Joe," in the foreground are three pairs of silver-colored, zero-length launchers for HVARs. Just beyond the inboard pair of launchers is the right pylon, capable of handling up to 1,000-pound bombs or drop tanks. Two of the teardrop-shaped counterweights of the right aileron are in view. *Author*

The lowered right flap of "Hairless Joe" is depicted, showing its three linkage hinges. The flaps are of a NACA (National Advisory Committee for Aeronautics) slotted-trailing-edge design. The end of the flap is closed off, with a sort of trusswork stamped into the metal for extra strength. *Author*

On the bottom of the outer part of the right wing are three identification lights: from front to rear, they have red, green, and amber lenses. On the leading edge of the wingtip is a clear fairing over a green-colored navigation light. The navigation light on the left side of the plane is red. *Author*

The aft end of the left pylon is viewed from its inboard side. The tube-shaped object on the rear of the pylon is a stabilizer bar, shown in its stored position. When a drop tank was mounted on the pylon, the stabilizer bar was swung down, to act as a brace against the rear part of the drop tank. *Author*

A zero-length launcher for the high-velocity aircraft rocket (HVAR) is seen close-up, with two other launchers arrayed to the other side of it. The HVARs had two clips for mounting the rockets to a front and a rear zero-length launcher. Zero-length launchers rendered unnecessary extended launchers, such as rail launchers or tube launchers. *Author*

The outboard part of the right main landing-gear bay is viewed, showing the upper part of the right main-gear oleo shock strut at the lower center. The cylinder in the bay at right angles to the main-gear strut is the main-gear retracting cylinder. To the lower right is a feature introduced to production starting with the P-47D-30-RE and P-47D-30-RA: a compressibility flap, one of which was on each side of the wing, to alleviate compressibility problems, principally sudden changes in control characteristics, during high-speed dives. *Author*

The right main landing gear is viewed from its inboard side. The extra-high-pressure cast-magnesium wheel with a drop-center rim is mounted on an oleo shock strut. The wheel has eight spokes. Sometimes a solid-disk cover was installed on the inboard side of the wheel. Retracting and lowering the main gear was actuated by hydraulic power. *Author*

In a view of the inboard end of the right main landing-gear bay, details are available for the inner landing-gear door. A bulge was designed into the door to provide clearance for the retracted wheel, and the unpainted panel on the door was typical for wartime P-47s. Attached to the front of the door is its actuating cylinder. To the right is the right engine exhaust. *Author*

At an airshow, "Hairless Joe" is parked next to a P-47 Thunderbolt nicknamed "Jacky's Revenge." On "Hairless Joe," two front zero-length launchers are visible between the pylon and the main landing gear: P-47D-40-RAs had provisions for two sets of these launchers at that location, in addition to the three sets of launchers outboard of the pylon. *Author*

"Hairless Joe" is seen at a different angle. Below the horizontal stabilizer is marked this plane's civil registration number, NX47DA. Below the rear of the wing root on the belly of the fuselage are four vertical-louver vents. *Author*

Toward the center of the photo, above the wing root and outlined in red, is the cover panel for the fuel filler, with a stencil above it indicating that the plane required aromatic fuels to a capacity of 100 US gallons. Above and to the rear of that access panel is a foldout handhold, to assist the pilot and ground crewmen when they climbed up onto the wing. Above the handhold is an access panel for the supercharger oil filler. *Author*

The small hole on the top of the white invasion stripe under the left bar of the national insignia is for inserting a steel bar for lifting the rear of the aircraft. "LIFT" is stenciled in black above it. Above the tail number on the vertical fin are the right antennas for the AN/APS-13 tail-warning radar. This radar set off an alarm when an enemy plane was approaching from the rear. *Author*

The tailwheel of "Hairless Joe" is viewed facing to the rear, showing the actuator for the right gear door. Fitted around the tailwheel strut is a boot, to keep foreign objects out of the gear bay. *Author*

The tailwheel is viewed from a closer vantage point. As was also the case with the main landing gear, it was necessary to closely monitor the tire pressure and adjust it according to the loads carried by the aircraft. *Author*

Both tail-gear-door actuators are visible in this detail photo of the tail gear. The actuators were mechanical links that drew the doors shut as the tail gear was retracted. *Author*

The tail-gear boot and the actuator rod for the left gear door are depicted. *Author*

In addition to providing a clear view of the lower part of the rudder, the rudder trim tab and actuator, and the taillight, this photograph shows the torque tube that connects the ailerons. The torque tube passes through a curved cutout in the rudder. *Author*

A photo of the left side of the empennage includes a view of the left antennas for the AN/APS-13 tail-warning radar, above the tail number. Also visible are the small flaps over the rudder hinges. *Author*

In a view of the left elevator and its trim tab, the elevator torque tube is visible on both sides of the rudder. The stencil to the right of the trim tab reads "TAB ADJUSTED AT FACTORY / DO NOT TOUCH." *Author*

The large stencil on the front of the tailwheel door reads "TAIL WHEEL / MOOR," while the small stencil on the rear of the door reads "TAIL WHEEL INFLATION / 50 P.S.I." The small access panel above the lift tube is for accessing the top of the tailwheel actuating cylinder. *Author*

In a photo of the left side of the fuselage of "Hairless Joe," the left intercooler door is at the center of the photograph. On the wing near the wing root is a black, non-slip-surface walkway. *Author*

The bubbletop canopy on the P-47D could be operated either electrically or manually. Electrical control was by means of a toggle switch. To open or close the canopy by hand, the pilot pulled inward on knobs inside the canopy and slid it to the desired location. *Author*

Visible through the open canopy of "Hairless Joe" is the K-14 gunsight, located behind the windscreen. This gunsight was equipped with a gyroscope, and it computed the correct lead for the target, as well as indicating the range. Also in view is the pilot's headrest, mounted on an armored plate to protect the head and shoulders from fire from behind. *Author*

The red, teardrop-shaped left navigation light is recessed in the leading edge of the wingtip, with a clear cover over it. On the underside of the wing is the retractable landing light. *Author*

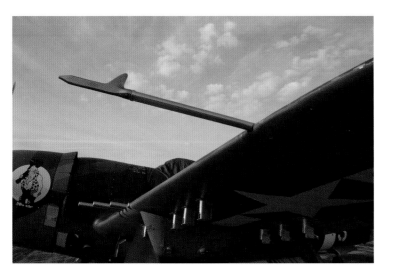

The pitot tube is on the leading edge of the left wing. This is a probe that is directed into the airflow to measure the airspeed. Farther inboard are the blast tubes for the left .50-caliber machine guns. *Author*

The same three rear zero-length launchers are viewed close-up. These launchers included clips to hold the rear mounting lugs (or, rear mounting suspension lug bands) on the rockets, and electrical connections for firing the rockets' motors. *Author*

The retractable landing light of "Hairless Joe" is viewed from a close perspective. Farther inboard are the rear zero-length launchers for the three sets of double launchers that are outboard of the pylon. *Author*

Each of the four Browning .50-caliber machine guns in each wing of the P-47 had a blast tube, into which the barrel of the gun fitted. The tubes were staggered to match the staggering of the guns within the wings. Even the outboard machine guns had blast tubes, enclosed within the wings. The blast tubes were designed in part to support the gun barrels, to absorb the blast of the powerful machine guns and protect the airframe. and to act as heat shields. *Author*

"NO-HAND-HOLD" is stenciled in black on the inboard blast tube on the left wing. All five forward zero-length launchers on that wing are visible from this angle. *Author*

The left inboard main landing-gear bay door is the focus of this photograph. The interior of the door and the landing-gear bay are coated in zinc chromate primer, of a yellowish-green color. The exception is the bare-metal panel on the upper part of the bay door. To the left is the left engine exhaust. *Author*

On the side of the fuselage adjacent to the cockpit is a scoreboard of *Balkenkreuze*, signifying "kills" of eighteen German aircraft. Farther forward is the plane's nomenclature and data stencil, giving the type and model of the aircraft (P-47D-40-RA), the USAAF serial number (44-90471), and other information. At the top are the names of the pilot of "Hairless Joe," Col. D. C. Schilling, and his crew chief, MSgt. Knudson. *Author*

The left main landing-gear doors linked to the oleo strut are seen from the outboard side. The lower door is marked at several places "NO STEP," to discourage ground crewmen from abusing the delicate door. At the bottom of the same door is a stencil indicating a jack position on the bottom of the main strut. *Author*

The left main landing gear and the two-part door linked to the oleo strut are viewed from the front. On the strut just above the tire is the scissors-type torque link. "TOW" is stenciled in black just above the top of the torque link. *Author*

Just aft of the cowling are, *left to right*, the left variable shutter for the oil-cooler exhaust; a fixed air deflector; and the left engine exhaust. The same elements are present on the right side of the aircraft. *Author*

The P-47Ds were powered by the Pratt & Whitney R-2800-59 Double Wasp eighteen-cylinder air-cooled radial engine. The dark-gray, bowl-shaped object at the front of the cylinders is the gear-reduction case. The propeller is the Hamilton Standard Hydromatic, drawing number 6507A-0, with the so-called paddle blades. The part number, serial number, and low and high pitch angles are stenciled in yellow on the blades. *Author*

"Hairless Joe" continues to carry on the tradition of the legendary P-47D Thunderbolts, giving crowds a rare glimpse of a still-flying "Jug" more than seventy years after the end of World War II. *Author*

CHAPTER 6
XP-47E, XP-47F, XP-47H, XP-47J, and XP-47K

As can be discerned from the preceding chapters, as the Thunderbolt design evolved, the basic "P-47" nomenclature was appended with various alphabetical suffixes denoting each new model. The nonexistent P-47A model was discussed in chapter 1, and the military routinely skipped "I" as being too difficult to distinguish from "1"—but what about all the other "missing" letters before the final model—the P-47N?

The designations XP-47E, XP-47F, XP-47H, XP-47J, and XP-47K were assigned to a series of experimental variants, as denoted by the X prefix, none of which went into series production.

The first of these, the XP-47E, was a 1942 experimental Thunderbolt with a pressurized cabin. Although the deliberate destruction of the Republic Aviation records by Fairchild Corporation in 1987 precludes the necessary archival research to ascertain with certainty whether or not any information gleaned from this experiment was incorporated in other aircraft, it appears that the experiment was for naught.

The XP-47F designation was applied to a P-47B that was modified with a new, laminar-flow wing. This was an effort to reduce drag, thereby increasing speed and range. First flown on September 17, 1942, the aircraft spent most of its life at the NACA facility at Langley, Virginia, before being lost in a crash on October 11, 1943.

The quest for more power seems to be as old as powered flight, and the XP-47H was an effort to bring more power to the Thunderbolt airframe. The engine selected to power the XP-47H was the 10-foot-long experimental Chrysler XIV-2220, a 2,500-horsepower inverted V-16 engine that held considerable promise. While the engine was first contracted for in July 1940, it would be July 1945 before the Thunderbolt with the engine installed first took flight. While the big Chrysler was a rare case of a new engine exceeding its forecast horsepower—the engine produced 3,000 horsepower in some tests—the modified Thunderbolt that the engine powered did not attain the 490 mph design speed. That, along with jet engines being the clear path to the future, meant that work on the XP-47H was abandoned.

With the "I" suffix being skipped, as explained earlier, the next variant was the XP-47J. This aircraft was intended to be a high-speed pursuit aircraft, featuring a fan-cooled R-2800-61 engine. Although attaining a top speed of 507 mph at 34,300 feet, and exceeding 500 mph on more than one occasion, the type did not go into series production.

The XP-47K began life as P-47D-5-RE serial number 42-8702 but was taken from the assembly line and extensively modified. The rear fuselage was cut down and the conventional canopy was removed. In its place, a new bubbletop canopy was placed over the cockpit, in an effort to improve all-important visibility for the pilot. This change, while causing a 3 percent loss of speed, provided the desired increase in visibility. Although no further P-47K aircraft were produced, the bubbletop canopy was introduced into P-47D production almost immediately after flight testing of the XP-47K.

Only one XP-47E-RE was built. This aircraft, which featured a pressurized cockpit for high-altitude operations, was converted by Republic from the P-47B-RE, serial number 41-6065. Completed in September 1942, the XP-47E was initially powered by a Pratt & Whitney R-2800-21 engine.
American Aviation Historical Society

After being delivered to Wright Field for testing, the Republic-applied chromate yellow paint scheme, typical of the company's experimental aircraft, was replaced by the standard Olive Drab and Neutral Gray two-color camouflage scheme. At the same time the engine was replaced as well, with an R-2800-59 rated at 2,300 horsepower. To accommodate this, the Curtiss Electric propeller was replaced with a Hamilton Standard unit, and a P-47D-style cowling was installed. *National Archives*

The sole XP-47F was created in an effort to reduce drag through the use of a NACA laminar-flow airfoil design. The new wing was also larger than that of Republic P-47B-RE, serial number 41-5938, from which it was converted. The aircraft, which was delivered in August 1942, was lost in a fatal crash on October 11, 1943. *National Museum of the United States Air Force*

The new wing is in place on this view of the XP-47F under construction at Republic's Farmingdale plant on June 25, 1942. The XP-47F was created to compare the performance of a P-47 with a NACA low-drag airfoil to the standard Thunderbolt wing, which had a Republic S-3 airfoil. *American Aviation Historical Society*

3/4 REAR VIEW (XP-47F) 6-25-42

Another view of the conversion work being done by Republic mechanics on June 25, 1942. The XP-47F flew for the first time on September 17, 1942, but did not go into serial production. *Roger Freeman collection*

The two experimental XP-47H aircraft were created by installing Chrysler XIV-2220 sixteen-cylinder, inverted-V, liquid-cooled engines in P-47D-15-RE airframes, serial numbers 42-23297 and 42-23298. In order to accommodate the 2,500-horsepower engines, the 1943 conversions involved a substantially modified and lengthened fuselage and the introduction of a chin-mounted radiator. This is the first XP-47H, just prior to its first flight. *American Aviation Historical Society*

The reduction gear of the Chrysler XIV-2220 was not at the front of the engine block, but at the center. A power shaft, just visible in this view of the sixteen-cylinder engine as installed on an XP-47H airframe, transmitted power to the propeller. Alongside the engine is its massive mount. *National Museum of the United States Air Force*

The initial flight tests of both XP-47Hs, such as this one flown by serial number 42-23297, were from the Evansville, Indiana, airport during the latter part of World War II. At the time of this flight the original flush compressor air intakes have been covered by protruding air scoops behind the canopy.
National Museum of the United States Air Force

While the other experimental Thunderbolts in this chapter were converted from P-47D airframes, the XP-47J was built new from the ground up. This aircraft was intended to be a very high-speed aircraft, coupling a powerful engine with a lightweight airframe. The engine was a Pratt & Whitney R-2800-57 (C) fan-cooled engine, and while it was intended to be fitted with a six-blade Aeroproducts contrarotating propeller, a conventional four-blade prop was used instead. *American Aviation Historical Society*

Behind the large propeller spinner and filling the front of the cowling is the engine-cooling fan. Below the cowling was the large air intake for the General Electric CH-5 turbosupercharger. The XP-47J first flew on November 26, 1943, and on August 4, 1944, set a new speed record for a propeller-driven plane of 504 mph. *National Museum of the United States Air Force*

The XP-47K was created as a test installation of a bubble canopy and a lower rear-fuselage deck in place of the standard razorback and conventional canopy. The XP-47K was converted from P-47D-5-RE, serial number 42-8702, and was completed in July 1943. *National Archives*

Although the P-47K did not enter production, that designation was stenciled on the vertical tail of the XP-47K. This aircraft utilized a modified bubble canopy from a British Hawker Typhoon. In addition to the new canopy, the XP-47K also featured an enlarged main fuselage fuel tank (now 270 gallons) and additional oxygen bottles. *San Diego Air and Space Museum*

CHAPTER 7
P-47M

The bubbletop Thunderbolt underwent further development in the P-47M, in which a Pratt & Whitney R-2800-57 engine raised horsepower (in war emergency setting) to 2,800, nearly 400 horsepower more than the P-47D-30 could deliver. With the new engine and also an improved Curtiss Electric C642S-B40 propeller, the P-47M hit speeds of 473 mph at 32,000 feet.

The upgrade showed great potential, and the Farmingdale plant began producing the new P-47Ms, which soon were rolling off the assembly line and arriving in Britain, starting on January 3, 1945. The veteran P-47 fliers of the 56th FG, based at RAF Boxted, took the new model into combat for the first time just a week and a half later, on January 14, and almost immediately problems appeared. The difficulties mostly concerned the new power plant—and often resulted in the engine stopping in midflight.

Because of the problems, the P-47Ms were grounded from February 26 to 28, 1945, and once again from March 16 to 24. In the end, the difficulties were found to stem from improper preservation of the engines prior to shipment—the saltwater environment of ocean transport caused the engines to deteriorate.

New engines were supplied by Pratt & Whitney, and soon the problems were solved. In the end, sixty-seven of the 130 P-47M aircraft manufactured found their way to Boxted.

Although there were relatively few P-47Ms and although their time in combat was rather limited, 56th FG pilots aboard the M Thunderbolts scored at least seven Axis aircraft destroyed in the air. Four of those were Germany's highly advanced jet-powered Messerschmitt Me 262s. In addition, P-47M fliers took out numerous other enemy aircraft in the course of ground attacks.

While the XP-47J was not placed in production, nevertheless a high-speed Thunderbolt was created to deal with the jet- and rocket-powered aircraft the Germans were deploying by 1944. While lacking the fan-cooling and large spinner of the XP-47J, the lightweight P-47M shared the Pratt & Whitney R-2800-57 C-series Double Wasp radial engine coupled with the new General Electric CH-5 turbosupercharger with the aborted design. Entering production late in the war, only one unit, the 62nd Fighter Squadron, 56th Fighter Group, would operate P-47Ms in combat. "Teddy," as P-47M-1-RE, serial number 44-21117, was known, was assigned to that unit. *Stan Piet collection*

Three YP-47M aircraft were built by Republic by converting P-47D-27-RE airframes. The three aircraft, serial numbers 42-27385, 42-27386, and 42-27388, were fitted with Pratt & Whitney R-2800-57(C) engines and CH-5 turbosuperchargers, thereby becoming the prototypes for the version. Also installed were new Curtiss Electric C642S-B40 propellers, featuring tapered blade cuffs that were wider toward the propeller hub. *National Museum of the United States Air Force*

All 130 P-47M-1-REs were built at Republic Aviation's home plant in Farmingdale, New York. The airframes were originally contracted for as the final 130 P-47D-30-REs. *National Museum of the United States Air Force*

Viewed from the right side, it is apparent that natural-metal P-47M-1-RE, serial number 44-21159, lacked the prominent dorsal fin or strake found on many of the P-47M-1-REs. The fins were installed at modification centers after the aircraft arrived in Europe. *National Museum of the United States Air Force*

With a smoke generator hung beneath its wing, P-47M-1-RE, serial number 44-21228, assigned to Maj.
Mike Quirk of the 62nd Fighter Squadron, 56th Fighter Group, passes over the English countryside.
National Museum of the United States Air Force

"Marion" was the nickname of the final P-47M-1-RE to be completed, serial number 44-21237. It was assigned to 2nd Lt. Walter J. Sharbo of the 62nd Fighter Squadron, 56th Fighter Group; this group was the only one to operate the P-47Ms in combat. The camouflage colors of the 62nd Fighter Squadron's P-47Ms reportedly were British Sea Gray and Dark Green, with bare-aluminum undersides and cockpit canopy frames. *Roger Freeman collection*

CHAPTER 8
P-47N

The vast expanses of the Pacific compelled the P-47D to push its range to its limit and beyond. The Army Air Force was loathe to let go of the Thunderbolt's power, and Republic Aviation was eager to preserve its lucrative arrangements with the military. Accordingly, a new variant of the Thunderbolt, one with increased range, was brought out.

The P-47N incorporated the powerful—and no-longer-problematic—R-2800-57 power plant from the P-47M and used the core fuselage of a P-47D-27 coupled with a totally new and longer wing. The P-47N's wingspan extended a full 42 feet, 10 inches. The squared-off tips of the wings also appreciably raised the roll rate. Additional fuel tanks were fitted into the inside of the longer wings, raising wing tank capacity to ninety-three gallons per wing. The ailerons on the outside of the new wings were longer; the flap area was now fifty percent greater than on the older-model wing.

When 300-gallon drop tanks were added under both wings, the P-47N could travel more than 2,000 miles at 25,000 feet, putting it in the same range category with the P-51 and P-38. The improved aircraft, of course, weighed more than previous Thunderbolts, but the new R-2800-57 engine gave the plane a top speed of 467 mph, a higher speed than any other production Thunderbolt other than the P-47M.

In all, 1,816 production P-47Ns were manufactured by Republic: 1,667 at Farmingdale, New York, and 149 in the plant at Evansville, Indiana. After the Japanese surrender, orders for a further 5,934 P-47Ns were canceled, and the model became the final Thunderbolt.

After the US Air Force separated from the US Army to become an independent branch of service, former pursuit planes were reclassified as fighters, and the "P" prefix was replaced with "F." All P-47Ns then in service thereby became F-47Ns. Any P-47D aircraft likewise became F-47Ds.

When the Korean War broke out in 1950, there were some calls to deploy Thunderbolts to that new conflict, but, since spare parts were lacking, none of the venerable planes were deployed to the war zone. All remained in service with Air National Guard units in the United States.

In the Pacific, the B-29 was able to bomb Japan from a considerable distance, leading to the need for long-range escort aircraft. In an attempt to fill that need, Republic Aviation created the XP-47N. Starting with the XP-47K, itself converted from P-47D-27-RE, serial number 42-27387, the company produced this aircraft, which featured redesigned wings of larger area with snubbed wingtips and enlarged flaps and ailerons, and an enlarged dorsal fin between the cockpit canopy and the vertical fin. Also included were fuel tanks totaling 93-gallon capacity in each wing, which when combined with other internal and drop tanks gave the aircraft a range of 2,350 miles. *National Archives*

The XP-47N, *right*, and an earlier P-47 are parked adjacent to each other to contrast the wing design. The P-47N had an 18-inch-wide extension at the root, blunt tips and were a combined 22 square feet larger than those of earlier-production Thunderbolts. *National Archives*

A Pratt & Whitney R-2800-57 C radial engine equipped with a General Electric CH-5 turbosupercharger powered the XP-47N. The XP-47N did not have the pronounced ventral fin on the longitudinal centerline between the rear of the cockpit canopy and the front of the tail fin, which, along with numerous internal changes, was a feature on the production aircraft. *National Archives*

The pylons of the P-47N had a capacity of up to 2,500 pounds in bombs. Beginning with the P-47N-5-RE production block, stub launchers for ten 5-inch rockets were added to the wings as well. These launchers were retrofitted to some earlier P-47N aircraft as well. *National Archives*

Because the 18-inch wing extensions were installed at the wing roots of the P-47N, the landing gear struts on these aircraft were farther apart than had been the case with earlier models.
American Aviation Historical Society

Hanging beneath the fuselage and visible between the main landing-gear struts of this P-47N-5-RE are sway braces used when mounting a bomb or a drop tank. Beneath the wings can be seen the stub launchers, arranged with three sets outboard of the bomb pylon and two sets inboard.
National Museum of the United States Air Force

Slightly different instrument panels were used throughout Thunderbolt production, sometimes with multiple versions even within a model. This view is typical for the P-47N. At right are the controls for cowl flaps and recognition lights. *National Museum of the United States Air Force*

The P-47M and P-47N were powered by the Pratt & Whitney R-2800-57 C-series radial engine. As seen on this cutaway display engine, the gear-reduction housing comprised two major parts: a drum with the cover fastened to the front with many screws. *National Museum of the United States Air Force*

The squadron assignment of this P-47N-1-RE, serial number 44-87800, is unknown. The cowl and dorsal fin appear to be painted dark orange or perhaps red, with matching stripes on the rudder.
Stan Piet collection

A P-47N with the insignia of the 1st Air Force on the cowl taxis past several US Navy aircraft sometime between 1945 and 1947. This aircraft has the type of wingtip navigation lights that predate the P-47N-25 production block. *Stan Piet collection*

The Thunderbolt was nearing the end of its service life when Republic F-47N-25-RE, serial number 44-89444, was photographed adjacent to a Convair F-102 Delta Dagger. This F-102 is just thirteen years newer than the F-47N. *National Museum of the United States Air Force*